frog face

~~ my little sister & me ~~

JOHN SCHINDEL   PHOTOGRAPHS BY **JANET DELANEY**

Henry Holt and Company • New York

First there was just me—Johanna—
just me and Mom and Dad.

Then one day they said a baby was on the way and I
was going to be a big sister. Sometimes I thought
being a big sister would be fun. And sometimes I
thought it wouldn't be fun and that Mom and Dad
didn't need to have anyone around but me.

Then she came.

My itty-bitty, goofy-looking but sort of cute,
squishy baby sister, Jillian. She made funny noises
and slept a lot and cried a lot and spit up and
pooped and peed a lot . . .

. . . and spent too much time with Mom.

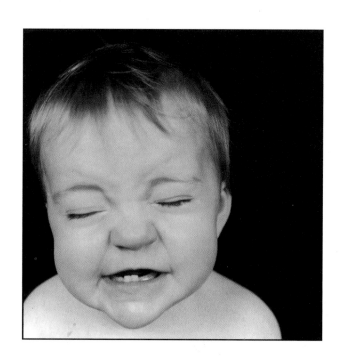

I called her frog face,   cry baby,

silly stinky bottom,

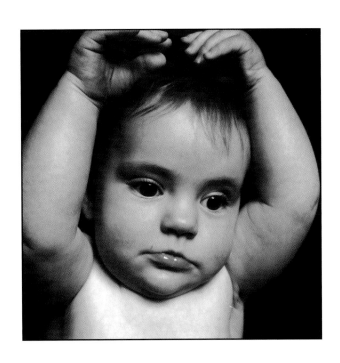 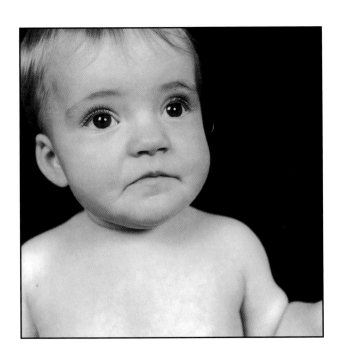

but she didn't care or understand.   She just stared at me.

But if I smiled, she smiled too!
I think I started smiling more when Jillian came.

Maybe having a little sister was going to be okay.

When she got a little older, I played with Jillian
and showed her how to do things.

But sometimes she'd do whatever she wanted,
like play with my toys when I didn't want her to.

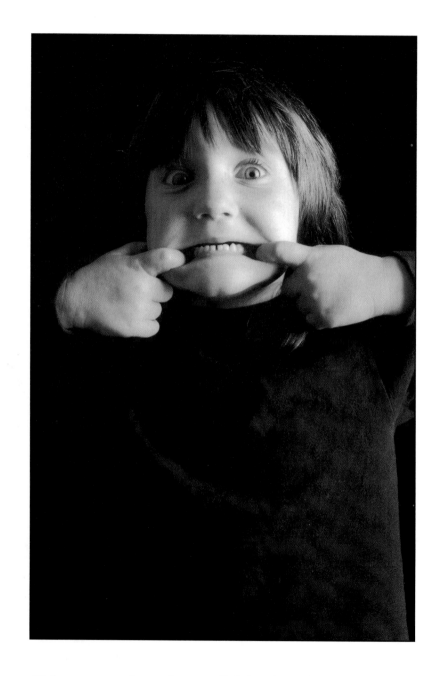

I'd get mad and say, "GO AWAY!"

Then one day she stopped talking baby talk and said,
"You go way!" Little sisters love to copy.

She liked to do whatever I did,

sometimes even the naughty things.

Always the fun things.

But she wasn't just like me—

there's only one me—

and Jillian is Jillian.

Sometimes Jillian does things by herself and I do things by myself. But we also do stuff together. Nobody says we have to. We want to.

We do things that big sisters and little sisters
can do because being sisters is special.

Mom says a sister is someone you can always be close to.
A sister is someone to love.

One year on Halloween, Jillian got
seventeen Hershey's Kisses and I only got six,
so she gave me four of hers.

She just did it. I didn't even ask.

That Thanksgiving we each made a wish and snapped the turkey wishbone. I got the bigger piece. That was supposed to mean that my wish would come true and Jillian's wouldn't. She cried, but I told her everything was going to be okay, because part of my wish was that her wish would come true too.

Jillian's lucky that I'm her sister. And even though we don't get along all the time and sometimes I want to sit on her, I'm lucky she's mine.

For my daughters, Celia and Nina — J. S.

For my daughters, Johanna and Jillian — J. D.

Henry Holt and Company, Inc., *Publishers since 1866*, 115 West 18th Street, New York, New York 10011
Henry Holt is a registered trademark of Henry Holt and Company, Inc.

Published in Canada by Fitzhenry & Whiteside Ltd., 195 Allstate Parkway, Markham, Ontario L3R 4T8.

Library of Congress Cataloging-in-Publication Data
Schindel, John. Frog face / John Schindel; photographs by Janet Delaney.
Summary: A girl describes the joys and frustrations of living with her little sister. [1. Sisters—Fiction.]
I. Delaney, Janet, ill. II. Title. PZ7.S34632Fr 1998 [E]—dc21 97-38300

ISBN 0-8050-5546-0 First Edition—1998 Typography by Meredith Baldwin
Printed in the United States of America on acid-free paper. ∞ 10 9 8 7 6 5 4 3 2 1
The artist used chromogenic and silver gelatin prints to create the photographs for this book.